SOLAR SYSTEM MARKETING®

SOLAR SYSTEM MARKETING

Marketing reimagined for *people* who are the brand

- Nina Christian -

A catalogue record for this book is available from the National Library of Australia

First published in 2026 by Starlight Press Melbourne, Australia

Editing by Alex Hagan
Cover concept by Nina Christian

For information about this title, contact:
Nina Christian
support@ninachristian.com
www.ninachristian.com

ISBN 978-1-7646220-0-4

DEDICATION

*For Alex, who was beside me at the planetarium
where this all began, and who I get to
build with every day.*

*For the clients who took to this way of thinking so
quickly and so naturally that they confirmed what I
felt the first time I used it: this works.*

*And for everyone with a message that matters who
just needs a simpler way to share it.*

*I hope this gives you the clarity and confidence to
share your message further and wider than
you ever thought possible. And that it makes the
doing of it simple, enjoyable, and a natural extension
of who you already are.*

Contents

PART I: INTRODUCTION **11**

Marketing for People Brands 13

Why Solar System Marketing® 17

How to Use This Book...19

The Hidden Tax of Modern Marketing 23

From Chaos to Cosmos 27

How a Solar System Works....................................31

The Universe of You 35

PART II: THE SUN YOUR CORE FOCUS **37**

The Centre of It All 39

Two Sides of the Sun...42

The Constancy of the Sun 45

Pause and Check Your Sun 50

PART III: THE PLANETS YOUR ORBIT OF IDEAS........... **51**

What Makes a Planet?..55

The Dimensions of You... 59

What the Planets Do For You 61

Mapping Your Planets 63

PART IV: PLANETARY LENSES................................**71**

How to Use the Lenses 73

Mercury – The Messenger.............................. 75

Venus – The Attractor 79

Earth – The Grounded Centre 83

Mars – The Drive.. 87

Jupiter – The Amplifier.................................... 91

Saturn – The Architect 95

Uranus – The Innovator................................... 99

Neptune – The Dreamer.................................. 103

Pluto – The Transformer 105

Looking Outward 109

PART V: BEYOND THE PLANETS **111**

Eris & The Kuiper Belt – The Periphery.......................113

Constellations – The Personas 117

Moons – The Stabilisers 121

Wormholes – The Connection Points......................123

Flying Objects – The Distractions.............................125

Black Holes – The Cautionary Lens..........................129

PART VI: BRINGING IT BACK DOWN TO EARTH........**133**

What holds your Solar System Together.................135

Marketing Messaging 137

Conversations as Content 141

A Cadence, Not a Calendar 143

Check-Ins and Reviews 147

Aligning Impact and Opportunities...........149

The Living System 151

Setting It In Motion...155

APPENDIX 157

Next Steps & Resources....................................158

Acknowledgements 160

About the Author 162

PART I: INTRODUCTION

Marketing for People Brands

When I first began building my personal brand alongside running a business, I tried to apply the same frameworks I used for corporate and small business marketing. Strategy documents, campaign calendars, layers of planning… and it just didn't work. It was too heavy. Instead of giving me clarity, it left me with an infinite to-do list I never had the time or energy to finish.

That was when I knew I needed a different approach. One that gives you just the right amount of structure without being overwhelming to implement.

When *you* are the brand, the rules of marketing change.

Businesses can hire agencies, run campaigns, and build entire departments around strategy and execution. For most people, even highly talented, ambitious people, that kind of infrastructure just isn't realistic. And yet, their professional viability still depends on being seen and understood by the right people.

Whatever the context, the need is the same: *purposeful visibility.*

The challenge is that the core elements of marketing, robust strategy, creativity, and critical thinking, aren't overly difficult to understand in principle, but they're surprisingly hard to apply to yourself. It's much harder to see the whole picture when you're inside the frame.

The traditional frameworks of marketing such as the four P's (product, price, place, promotion), while timeless, can feel impossibly heavy for an individual to execute. They make sense in theory, but in practice they stay stuck on an endless to-do list.

What personal brands need is 'just enough' marketing, not overblown frameworks. Because a person isn't an organisation. You don't have a team, a budget, or a department. You have yourself, your ideas, and a limited number of hours.

You might think you need lots of marketing experience to build a captivating personal brand. This simply isn't true. Finding what makes you unique and how to express that in the world is something best done by you. Anyone can build a compelling personal brand when they have the right tools and processes.

The hardest part is being extraordinary at what you do, knowing what you're called to do, and having a passion to lean into it and make it real. This book will help you with the rest.

My first book, *Marketing Me*, is a comprehensive look at personal branding and marketing for people-owned brands, with a strong lens on understanding and articulating the identity set at the heart of a magnetic personal brand. You don't need to have read it before reading this one, but they work well together.

Solar System Marketing® is a deeper dive into what to do once you know who you are: a strategic framework for consistently putting your message into the world without being repetitive.

It's the practical system for getting seen in a way that's sustainable, strategic, and unmistakably you. Simple, visual, and powerful enough to help you clarify your focus and amplify your presence, without needing a marketing department to make it happen.

Why Solar System Marketing®

When I wrote *Marketing Me*, I focused on helping people uncover and embrace their identity as a brand. But I kept hearing the same question: *"I know who I am now, but what do I actually talk about? And how do I keep showing up without burning out, or being boring?"*

Solar System Marketing® is my answer to that question.

When you start to see yourself as a universe, with galaxies, solar systems, and a Sun, it becomes clear why traditional marketing models feel so heavy. Those models weren't designed for people, but for organisations with teams, budgets, and departments.

What individuals need is something simpler that gives them amplification, alignment and attraction, without being overwhelming to execute.

That's what Solar System Marketing® is. A practical framework built around strategy, creativity, and critical thinking, that honours our complexity, but gives us clarity and helps us move forward without overthinking... A framework that turns timeless principles into something we can actually work with.

Whether you're a consultant, an expert, a professional building visibility inside your organisation, or a founder without a full marketing team[1], it will meet you where you are.

This book will give you a framework to:

- **Clarify your Sun:** your core commercial focus.

- **Identify your planets:** your key concepts, messages and ideas.

- **Work with natural forces of attraction, amplification, and alignment** so your presence feels more easeful, rhythmic, and coherent.

You'll discover that when your system is clear, marketing stops feeling like effort and starts feeling like expression.

---

[1] *While the focus is on people-led brands, the framework also brings clarity to small teams who have overcomplicated things and need more potency and freshness in their message.*

How to Use This Book

This is a deliberately short book. You can read it in one sitting and take in the whole idea, or dip in and out as you wish.

The most important thing is that you start with the Sun. Once you've identified your current focus, you can skim or dive deeper into the planets and beyond.

There's a subconscious unlock that happens when you let ideas sit for one to three days. This sharpens the potency because it's not just about understanding the ideas intellectually; it's about feeling them. If you don't *feel* them, they won't carry the same resonance.

For that reason, I recommend two ways to move through this book:

a. All in one sitting, in two rounds. Read it through in a single session, see what ideas surface, let it settle for one to three days, and then come back to it again.

or

b. Read Part 1 in the first sitting, then explore the Sun, the planets, and the sections beyond one at a time. Give yourself 15 minutes each day to reflect on just one section. Think of it like a devotional practice, a daily lens that opens something new.

Whichever way you choose, along the way you're going to learn some fascinating facts about astronomy, mythology, and yourself.

In the last part of the book, you'll find a section on implementation with practical examples of how to apply Solar System Marketing® to your brand.

If you'd like to, you can also download a free companion kit at SolarSystemMarketing.com to work through as you read this book and note the decisions and ideas that surface along the way.

A Practical Companion

This framework is designed for more than just content. Yes, it can shape your blogs, posts, campaigns, and marketing strategy, but it also works in conversations, meetings, and the ways you naturally speak about what you're doing right now.

Each time you return to it, your IP will evolve, because you'll be expressing it in new ways.

But first, let's look at the problem the framework is actually solving.

The Hidden Tax of Modern Marketing

You sit down to create a piece of marketing content. You have thirty minutes before your next call. You open a blank document and think, *What should I write about today?* Ten ideas float through your mind. You start drafting one, then second-guess it. You pivot to another angle, write two sentences, delete them. You glance at what others in your space posted this morning and feel a knot form in your stomach. Fifteen minutes gone. You close the laptop and tell yourself you'll do it later. Later doesn't come.

If that feels familiar, you're not alone. It's the default experience for most people trying to market themselves, and it's the problem this book will help you solve.

Today's tools have made the mechanics of creating content easier than ever. In many ways, the "blank page friction" is gone. Prompts, templates, and AI drafting tools can get you to a first version in minutes.

AI has solved many of the problems of execution, but introduced a new one: the weight of infinite choice.

When you can say anything, how do you know what to say?

The paradox of choice, popularised by Barry Schwartz[2], is the concept that while our intuition tells us that having more options is better, in fact it works against us, so much so that we end up choosing nothing at all.

Beyond a certain point, an abundance of choice becomes overwhelming and counterproductive.

The pattern works like this:

- **Decision paralysis**. When faced with too many options, people often struggle to choose at all, or avoid deciding entirely. The more choices, the harder it is to commit.

- **Opportunity cost.** Every option you pick means rejecting all the others. The more alternatives exist, the more you're aware of what you're giving up, which erodes satisfaction with your choice.

- **Rising expectations.** More options raise the bar for what a "perfect" choice looks like. If

---

[2] *Barry Schwartz, The Paradox of Choice: Why More Is Less (2004)*

there are 100 options, surely one of them must be ideal, and if your pick falls short, it feels like your fault for not choosing better.

- **Regret and second-guessing.** After choosing, you're more likely to wonder "what if?" when you know dozens of alternatives existed.

A classic real-world example is a study involving jam by Sheena Iyengar and Mark Lepper[3]: shoppers were more likely to buy jam when presented with 6 varieties than when presented with 24, even though the larger display attracted more initial interest.

The takeaway isn't that choice is bad, but that there's a sweet spot. Enough options to feel autonomous, but not so many that the decision itself becomes a burden.

When everything is possible, nothing feels clear, and we end up stuck, overwhelmed, or making no decision at all.

This is the hidden tax of the modern marketing era: *decision fatigue*. And it's why we need a simpler way,

---

[3] *Sheena Iyengar and Mark Lepper, "When Choice is Demotivating," Journal of Personality and Social Psychology, 2000*

a framework that removes the overwhelm of endless choice and gives us a natural system to follow.

That's where the move from chaos to cosmos begins.

From Chaos to Cosmos

The previous section diagnosed the hidden tax of decision fatigue. This chapter is where the cure begins, where we move from chaos to cosmos.

The word cosmos comes from the Greek *kosmos,* meaning order, harmony, a well-arranged system. Where chaos is scattered, cosmos is aligned. It suggests that things aren't random at all; there's a rhythm, a pattern, a way it all fits together.

Philosophers and scientists have long used "cosmos" to describe the universe as an ordered whole, a system with coherence and balance.

Sometimes, when we speak more expansively, cosmos evokes something larger: the vast, mysterious, interconnected beauty of everything.

When you move from chaos to cosmos in how you show up in the world. Instead of scattered effort, endless lists, and random acts of content, you'll discover how to bring order and flow to your brand. You'll do this by tapping into a natural system that already exists inside you, and learning to work with it.

Marketing Chaos vs. Marketing Cosmos

Chaos	Cosmos
Scattered effort	Centred Focus
Endless to-do lists	A clear cadence
Random acts of content	Content with gravitational pull
Busy but invisible	Visible with purpose
Lots said, little remembered	Clear mesage that resonates
Reactive and exhausting	Rhythmic and sustainable
Overthinking what to say	Knowing what orbits your sun

When you make this shift, something remarkable happens: your presence becomes more attractive, your message is amplified, and your work comes into alignment with what matters most.

Just as the cosmos is held together by invisible forces, your own system is held together by three:

- **Attraction:** how you draw in the right people. It's the reason someone lands on your website or your profile and thinks, *"This person gets it."* When your core message is clear and your energy is congruent, the right people find you without you having to chase them.

- **Amplification**: how your message reaches further. It's what happens when a single idea you share gets carried across platforms, conversations, and collaborations, travelling well beyond the room you first said it in.

- **Alignment:** how it all fits together. It's the difference between feeling like you're spinning twelve plates and feeling like everything you create feeds the same fire. When your work, your message, and your offers all point in the same direction, people trust you faster.

These three forces will weave through this book as undercurrents running beneath every idea, and we'll return to them at the end. Because when they work together, your scattered energy gathers into a living cosmos: ordered, radiant, and alive.

How a Solar System Works

If you've ever stood outside on a clear night, away from the city, and looked up, you know the feeling. I love doing this when I'm on the beach just after sunset. That slow breath as your eyes take in the colour then gradually adjust as the the night sky fills in. First a handful of stars, then hundreds, then thousands.

The universe is vast and ever-expanding, filled with countless galaxies. Within each galaxy are solar systems: stars with planets, moons, and comets, all bound together by the gravity of the star they orbit. Every galaxy has its own character, and every solar system has its own order, held in place by the star at its centre.

In a way, you're a universe too. Full of different galaxies, the domains of your life and work. Some are personal, others are professional. Each galaxy represents an area of lived experience, depth, and authority. Places you can speak and lead from with substance.

If you're a leadership consultant who also mentors young founders and runs a wellness practice on the side, those are three different galaxies. They each have their own language, their own audience, their own weight. You don't have to choose just one to exist as a person. You *do* need to know which one you're operating in when you're building your brand.

Inside those galaxies are solar systems. Each has its own 'sun'[4], the central focus that gives light, warmth, and gravity, holding everything else together.

Within your leadership galaxy, for instance, you might have several possible solar systems: executive coaching, team culture, leadership in times of change. Each could be a centre of gravity in its own right. But only one can be the one you're shining your brightest light on right now.

That's the Sun.

In Solar System Marketing®, your Sun is your current commercial focus. If someone asked, "What do you do?", your Sun is the one sentence you'd want them to repeat accurately a week later.

---

[4] *In astronomy, a solar system technically refers to our Sun and the bodies orbiting it, while other stars with orbiting planets are called planetary systems. For simplicity, I use "solar system" throughout this book to describe any star with its orbiting bodies.*

Around your Sun orbit your planets: the key ideas, themes, and messages that make your work distinctive and recognisable. We'll get to those soon. For now, let's stay with the bigger picture.

My Universe in Practice

In my own universe, there are galaxies of entrepreneurship, parenting, mentoring, wellbeing, leadership, marketing, gardening, and a few others.

My personal purpose is to help people have more impact and live into their purpose. It's just who I am, and I could connect that purpose to how I approach almost any domain.

Within my professional galaxy of marketing, there are many possible solar systems: B2B marketing, running an agency, training young marketers, marketing technology, or personal branding. Each of these could have been its own solar system, with a Sun at the centre and ideas orbiting around it.

Right now, the solar system I've chosen to focus on is personal branding. My Sun, at the time of writing, is helping people build future-ready brands.

Knowing this gives coherence to everything I create and share, and it pulls my whole system into alignment.

That's how it looks in my world. Now, let's turn the lens to you.

The Universe of You

Every person is a universe, full of galaxies. Each galaxy holds a different domain of your life and work: a sphere where you've lived, learned, and gained depth. Some are personal, others professional. Together, they form a whole that is uniquely yours.

But you don't need to map your entire universe. Instead, let's choose one solar system and build around it.

Your solar system is your commercial focus. It sits within one of your galaxies and contains everything that makes your professional brand coherent: your Sun at the centre, your planets orbiting around it, and the forces that hold it all together.

You may draw on other galaxies from time to time. A personal story, a lesson from a completely different domain. That's natural, and it can add richness. The solar system simply gives you a home base, so those wider references have somewhere to land.

When your solar system is clear, people know what you do. They know what to come to you for. They know what to refer you for. And your marketing feels like it has a centre of gravity rather than a long list of things you could say.

So before we go deeper into the Sun itself in the next chapter, take a moment here.

Reflection

What galaxies (roles, interests, domains of knowledge) exist in the universe of you?
List them, personal and professional.

Which galaxy holds the solar system (focus of your personal brand) you're looking to build right now?
If you're not sure, then which one is your current commercial focus?

If you had to name your Sun in one sentence, what would it be? (What's at the centre? What gives energy and illumination to everything in that solar system?)

PART II: THE SUN

YOUR CORE FOCUS

The Centre of It All

Let me tell you about a pattern I see all the time.

Someone comes to me with brilliant content. They're creating content regularly, sharing smart ideas, showing up with energy and generosity. But when I look at their feed, or have an in-person conversation with them, or hear them speak on a podcast, I can't tell what they do. I can't tell who it's for. I assume their audience feels the same way: impressed, maybe, but unsure what to do next. One post is about leadership, the next on resilience, then a hot take on AI, then something about morning routines. Each piece is high quality, but they're not reinforcing one another.

The effort is there. The return isn't.

But this pattern doesn't only show up in people who are just starting out.

Chris Green is an extraordinarily successful coach who has guided businesses from startup to hundreds of millions in revenue. When we mapped his solar system together, we weren't looking for something he was missing so much as something he hadn't yet named. Working through his body of work — his programmes, his books, his speaking, everything he had built over decades — a single thread emerged running beneath all of it: he helps people unlock potential by breaking through barriers. Everything he had ever done said that, without ever quite saying it.

When Chris saw it, his face lit up. *"I've been trying to figure out that messaging for years,"* he said. *"It's exactly right. I'm putting it on my website tomorrow."*

That clarity didn't just give him better words. It gave him energy, gravity, and a centre that his audience could finally feel and point to. Once his Sun was named, the people around him could finally point at it. They knew what to come to him for. They knew what to refer others to him for.

When I ask people at any stage of their career, *"What's the one thing you want people to know you for right now?"*, the answer is usually a long pause, followed by a list. I get it. Most of us can do more than one thing well. But the irony is that being known for many things often means being chosen for none.

On the other hand, when you're known for one compelling thing, many doors open. Your audience doesn't need to see all of you at once. They need a centre of gravity, something that holds everything together and makes sense of what you're putting out into the world.

For Chris, that was a simple phrase that drew together everything he'd done and everything he's passionate about – unlocking potential by breaking through barriers.

That centre is Chris's Sun, and you'll have your own

It provides light, warmth, and the gravity that holds everything together. The Sun is what makes the planets' orbits possible and life sustainable. It is the centre, the anchor, the source of energy.

In the same way, your professional life also needs a Sun. Without one, your presence scatters. Your ideas and content may be bright, but without a centre of gravity they drift, disconnected and difficult for others to follow. When your Sun is clear, everything else finds its rightful orbit.

Two Sides of the Sun

In Solar System Marketing®, the Sun represents two things at once. First, it is your **commercial focus**: what people can buy from you now. This might be your service, your product, your book, or your program. It is the point where all your content should eventually land, the centre of gravity that makes your marketing commercially viable.

The Sun is also your **essence**: the part of you that shines through in everything you do, no matter what season you are in or which offer you are selling. Your energy, your voice, your way of seeing the world. These infuse your content naturally, and they matter as much as your commercial focus.

This dual nature is what gives your Sun its power. It's what you're selling and *who you are while you're selling it*. Both at once. Together, they make your presence magnetic.

The Pull of Gravity

Just as the Sun's gravity keeps planets from flying off into space, your commercial focus keeps your content from drifting into irrelevance. A well-defined

Sun reduces decision fatigue. You don't have to second-guess every idea. You simply ask: Does this orbit back to my Sun? If the answer is yes, it belongs in your system. If no, it's a distraction.

That same clarity acts as a filter for everything else too. You don't need to evaluate every new trend or opportunity from scratch. The question is always the same: does this orbit my Sun? If not, it's not for this season. That single question protects your energy and keeps your business on course.

This clarity makes your message kinder to your audience too. People don't have to work hard to understand who you are or what you stand for. **Clear is kind. Clear is commercial.**

A Question of Alignment

Finding your Sun means bringing together what you're offering right now with what you want to be known for in the long term. It's both commercial and positional.

If it's only short-term, it risks being unsustainable. If it's only aspirational, it risks being vague. The sweet spot lies in the alignment of both.

So ask yourself:

What am I selling or offering right now? What essence of me always shines through? If my clients had to describe me in one line, what would they say?

Your answers will help you clarify your Sun. If someone encounters your work a few times — reads your posts, chats with you at an event, listens to you speak somewhere — and still cannot easily tell what you do or who it's for, your Sun is not clear yet.

To make this more concrete: imagine a leadership coach whose commercial offer is a twelve-week executive presence program. Her essence is directness, warmth, and a knack for cutting through corporate fluff. Her Sun might be: "helping senior leaders communicate with clarity and confidence." That's specific enough to guide her content, broad enough to sustain a body of work, and true to who she is.

Now compare that with someone whose Sun is simply "leadership." That's a galaxy, not a Sun. It's too wide to orbit. Your Sun needs enough specificity that your audience can feel its pull.

The Constancy of the Sun

The Sun doesn't move toward us or away from us. It simply *is* — steady, unwavering, the fixed point that everything else organises around. Its constancy is what makes life possible.

In the same way, your professional Sun brings reliability and coherence to your brand. When people know what you stand for and see you consistently show up in that light, they begin to trust you.

When you feel pulled in too many directions, chasing trends, or drowning in ideas, your Sun is the place you return to. You pause and ask: *Does this idea orbit back to my Sun? Am I making it easy for people to understand what I'm about?*

This simple act of checking in re-orients you, restores your clarity, and brings your world back into coherence.

A Regular Review

To stay aligned, I recommend a simple ritual: a quarterly or half-yearly Sun Review.

Ask yourself:

Does my current Sun still reflect my essence?

Is it aligned with what I am selling now?

Does it build towards the reputation I want long-term?

What has changed in my energy, my offers, or my market that might call for adjustment?

Visibility and Trust

When your Sun is clear, others feel it, even before they fully understand what you do. They sense direction. Something about your presence makes sense to them, even if they can't articulate why.

The Sun illuminates. It makes things visible. In your work, your Sun shines a clear light on what you do, how you help people, and why it matters. It allows others to see the value of your expertise without having to search for clues. When your Sun is well defined, every story, every example, every idea points back to a central light source. Your audience comes to rely on you for clarity and direction. They don't have to guess. They can see what you stand for.

The Sun is more than bright, though. It's warm. Its heat is what sustains growth on Earth, and its presence makes life feel possible. Your Sun has the same effect on your audience. When your focus is clear and you communicate it with warmth, people feel safe in your light. They know what to come to you for. They feel comfortable recommending you because the words are easy: *"Go to them for X, they're brilliant at Y."*

Visibility and trust aren't separate things. They feed each other. The clearer your Sun, the warmer it feels.

A Simple Test

Try this: share your Sun with someone who doesn't know your work well. If they can describe it back to you in their own words and it still sounds accurate, you're on the right track.

If they look confused, or reflect back something that doesn't feel like you, that's useful information too. It means your Sun might need sharpening, or the way you're communicating it needs refinement.

Your Sun is only as powerful as its clarity. When others can see it, feel it, and describe it, you know it's doing its job.

When to Pivot vs. Launch a New Solar System

When to pivot your Sun: Your essence is the same, but your commercial expression needs an update. Example: moving from coaching individuals to consulting to organisations.

How you know: you still light up when you talk about the same core topic, but the way you deliver it or the audience you deliver it to has shifted. The thread is continuous, even if the shape of the offer looks different.

When to launch a new solar system: You are building a focus that sits in an entirely different galaxy. Example: if your Sun has been about leadership consulting, but you now want to focus on artisan food design, that belongs in a new system altogether.

How you know: when you try to connect the new thing back to your existing Sun, it feels forced. You find yourself constantly explaining the link. If the bridge between the two requires a paragraph of justification, you're probably looking at a new solar system.

Think of it this way. Pivots are seasonal adjustments to your Sun. New solar systems are new creations in your wider universe.

Pause and Check Your Sun

Before you move on, make sure you can do this:

- State your Sun in a single sentence. One clear line that captures your core commercial focus.

- Share that sentence with someone outside your world and have them understand it without needing you to explain further.

- Write three different ways you might communicate your Sun: one for a social post, one for a conversation, one for your website or bio.

If you can do all three, your Sun is doing its job.

Your Sun holds everything together. A solar system with only a Sun is just a star, though. Next, we map what orbits it.

PART III: THE PLANETS

YOUR ORBIT OF IDEAS

Your Orbit of Ideas

In Solar System Marketing®, planets are the big ideas that orbit your Sun — distinct angles on your core commercial focus, each one a theme you can speak to with depth, lived experience, and substance. Without them, you risk shining brightly but one-dimensionally.

The Sun is what makes your system *strategic*; the planets are what make it *dynamic*.

This is why your system needs more than a single focus. It needs an orbit of ideas: themes that are distinct enough to stand on their own, but close enough to stay aligned with your Sun. Together, they give you the variety your audience craves, without scattering your energy.

Planets aren't "extra topics" you have to create. They're the natural expressions of your lived experience and expertise. They're already in you. This framework simply helps you name them, organise them, and work with them intentionally.

Think of your planets as your orbit in action. Instead of asking "What should I say today?" you simply move through them, one at a time, each one offering a fresh angle on your Sun.

It's time to stop circling your ideas and start putting them into orbit.

Over the next chapters, you'll:

- Discover the criteria that make an idea "planet-worthy."

- Understand how your planets express the many dimensions of you.

- Map your own set of planets with a clear, simple process.

By the end of this part, you'll have a solar system that is unmistakably yours: a living framework you can return to again and again, to anchor your ideas and renew your voice.

Reflection

When you talk about your work, what themes come up again and again? Don't try to sift and sort here. Grab a notebook, let your mind run free and list whatever comes up for you.

Which ideas feel like they're always orbiting around your main focus, even when you're not trying?

What Makes a Planet?

In 2006, astronomers did something that upset a generation of schoolchildren: they fired Pluto. For decades, Pluto had a seat at the table. Then scientists asked a harder question: *what actually makes a planet?*

Not every object in the sky counts. Space is full of fragments: asteroids, meteors, comets. Pieces of rock and ice that pass through but don't carry enough weight to hold their place in orbit. A true planet is different. It has mass, gravity, and presence. It's stable enough to stay, and significant enough to shape the system around it. Pluto, beloved as it was, couldn't meet the bar.

The same is true for your brand. Not every idea, story, or angle deserves planet status. Some are passing sparks, fun experiments, or shiny distractions — useful in the moment but not central to your orbit. A planet has to earn its place.

The Criteria for a Planet

For an idea to qualify as a planet in Solar System Marketing®, it needs three things:

Gravity

A planet has enough weight to matter. In your brand, that means the theme has substance. You can talk about it with depth, credibility, and lived experience. It's not just a passing thought.

Orbit

A planet only belongs in your system if it orbits your Sun. In professional terms: does this idea reinforce your core commercial focus? If not, it's probably an asteroid. Interesting, but not a planet.

Essence

A planet only comes alive when it carries your voice. Otherwise it's just a dead rock floating in space. Infused with your essence, it becomes a living, breathing theme that feels recognisably you, even when others talk about similar ideas.

When you know what belongs, you stop leaking time and energy on what doesn't.

Your planets are a way of gathering what's already inside you and putting it in orbit. They give you clarity, and your energy flows toward what matters, while passing sparks can drift by like comets without disrupting your system.

When you know what counts as a planet, you stop trying to turn every passing idea into a pillar. You can enjoy playing with shiny thoughts, trends, or emerging ideas without mistaking them for something that should anchor your system.

Reflection

Take a look at the themes you brainstormed in the previous chapter.

Which ideas have real gravity? The ones you could speak about with authority and depth?

Which of those ideas clearly connect back to your Sun, your current commercial focus?

Which themes come alive because of the way you express them, different to how others might approach the same topic?

The Dimensions of You

Anyone can write about leadership, innovation, or branding. But when those ideas are filtered through your lived experience, your voice, and your perspective, they stop being generic and start becoming magnetic.

Generally speaking, people don't follow topics. They follow people who make topics feel relevant, personal, and real.

Your audience is hungry for depth. They don't want content that could have been written by anyone. They want to feel *you* in every piece.

The planets give you a way to show your depth and nuance without overwhelming yourself or your audience.

And when your planets are clear, something shifts: you stop second-guessing whether your content hangs together, because you can see that it does.

The Sun holds it. The planets express it.

Reflection

Which themes feel most alive when you infuse them with your voice and perspective?

Where do you notice yourself naturally adding depth, story, or a distinctive angle?

What the Planets Do For You

If you've ever stared at a blank page wondering what to say next, it probably wasn't because you had nothing. It was because you had too much. Endless possibility, as we looked at earlier, can be just as paralysing as a blank page.

The planets dissolve that paralysis.

They take the scattered brilliance of your ideas and organise them into a living system: one that serves both your short-term focus and your long-term positioning.

The planets give you categories, filters, and themes.

By rotating through your planets, you create variety without confusion. Your audience experiences you as both consistent **and** multi-dimensional. You experience yourself as clear and grounded.

Over time, this rhythm builds momentum. Your planets become familiar themes your audience recognises and associates with your brand. They hear your voice echoing through different angles, but it all still comes back to the Sun.

A defined orbit gives you more creative range, not less. You can explore each planet from dozens of angles, tell different stories within each one, go deep or go light. The structure holds you, so the creativity can breathe.

Mapping Your Planets

Now it's time to put **your** orbit on paper.

How Many Planets?

A common question is: how many planets should you have? While there's no fixed rule, I've found the sweet spot is usually between seven and ten. This gives you enough variety to keep things fresh, while still maintaining coherence. If you only have four or five, you may find yourself short on depth and range. If you stretch beyond twelve, you risk fragmentation.

There are exceptions, of course. But if you're starting out, aim for that seven-to-ten zone. It's long enough to rotate over a couple of months so you don't feel repetitive, and short enough to stay cohesive and memorable.

The Mapping Process

What does this actually look like? Grab a blank page, a whiteboard, or even a set of sticky notes on your desk. My personal favourite is a blank A3 sheet of paper and coloured markers.

Draw your Sun in the middle and write your Sun statement inside it. Then draw some individual circles around your Sun. Leave space inside them for the planets you're about to identify. Some people draw concentric rings. Some use sticky notes so they can move things around. Some open a blank slide in a graphics app or a notes app. The format doesn't matter.

What's important is that you can see your whole system in one place. There's something that clicks when you look at your Sun surrounded by your planets. It stops feeling abstract and starts feeling like something you can actually work with.

Now we go through a simple process to identify and map your planets:

Step 1: Brainstorm freely

Return to the reflection questions from earlier chapters. *What themes keep showing up? What do you talk about naturally? What topics do people associate with you?*

Write down everything that comes to mind without filtering. You're looking for the big themes and ideas that keep showing up in your work. The ones you return to again and again.

Step 2: Apply the criteria

For each idea on your list, ask:

Does it have gravity? *Can I speak about this with depth and lived experience?*

Does it orbit my Sun? *Does it reinforce my current commercial focus?*

Does it carry my essence? *Does it feel like me when I talk about it?*

If an idea doesn't meet all three criteria, it's not a planet. It might be an asteroid (a one-off piece of content) or a comet (a passing interest).
That's fine. Let it drift by.

Step 3: Name your planets

For the ideas that pass the test, give each one a clear, simple name. This becomes the shorthand you'll use when planning content. For example: "Storytelling," "The power of simplicity," "Authentic leadership," "Systems for sustainability."

Step 4: Add depth

For each planet, jot down one sentence that captures what it means to you, or three to four dot points that filter it through your dimension and bring its essence to life.

Step 5: Visualise your system

Arrange your Sun at the centre and your planets in orbit around it. This becomes your solar system map: simple, visual, and ready to use.

One more thing before you move on. If you've worked through these steps and some of your planets feel clear while others remain elusive, that's completely normal. The planetary lenses in the next section can help.

Each lens — drawn from the nine planets in our solar system — carries a distinct quality that may help you to find words for something you already knew but hadn't yet articulated. Some people find their planets through reflection. Others find them by holding a lens up to their work and suddenly seeing what was always there.

To help you with this process, you can download the Solar System Marketing® worksheet at SolarSystemMarketing.com. On one page, you'll map your Sun and your planets, creating a visual map you can return to whenever you need direction.

You can also have Virtually Myself® analyse your full scope of IP and map your solar system for you at www.virtuallymyself.com.

Example: My Solar System in Practice

Here's how this might look in practice using my own solar system at the time of writing.

My Sun:

Building a future-ready personal brand with soul and strategy

My Planets:

Clarity as Strategy - When you're clear, less does more. The antidote to overthinking, overcomplicating and overproducing. And the most commercial move you can make.

Radical Congruence - When who you are and how you show up are in full alignment, trust follows naturally. The new currency of personal branding.

Define Your Category - How to position yourself not just as a choice, but the *premium* choice. Where trust, authority and reputation compound until you're the one others are measured against.

Lead with Identity – People connect with what makes you unique. Your quirks, passions and perspectives are your competitive advantage.

The Expert's Ecosystem™ - Create your self-reinforcing system where your positioning, content and visibility all work together, so you build momentum with every interaction.

Strategic Storytelling - Why stories stick when information fades. How to find and tell the stories with visual vitality that make your brand memorable.

Simple Systems and Structures - How to create sustainability and amplification without overwhelm. Making marketing feel spacious rather than frantic.

The Inner Game of Confidence - The mindset and self-trust required to show up consistently. Navigating fear, doubt, and the vulnerability of being seen.

Amplification with Intention - How to extend your reach and discoverability without diluting what makes you distinctive.

The Human Brand - When you are the brand, your capacity, energy and wellbeing are business assets. Protecting them is strategy.

Each of these planets orbits the same Sun: *Building a future-ready personal brand with soul and strategy.* But each one offers a different angle, a different conversation, a different way in. Together, they create a rich, dynamic presence that enable me to stay coherent without becoming repetitive.

Your Turn

Take some time now to map your own solar system. Start with your Sun, then identify the planets that naturally orbit it. Remember: they're already in you. This process is simply about naming them and putting them in order.

PART IV: PLANETARY LENSES

How to Use the Lenses

You've mapped your solar system. You have a Sun and a set of planets that orbit it with purpose. For some of you, the lenses ahead will do something else entirely: they may surface a planet you didn't know you had, or give a name to something that has always been present in your work but never quite articulated.

For those whose orbit is already clear, the lenses offer a different gift: fresh angles on the themes you already own. A planet that felt familiar during mapping may surprise you when you hold it up to a different light. As you move through the lenses, they'll start to layer. By the time you've explored two or three, you'll have enough range to build a full content sprint from a single planet. By the end, you won't just understand your orbit. You'll know how to keep it spinning.

Either way, these aren't new planets to add. They're perspectives borrowed from the sky — nine distinct qualities that help you see your Sun and your existing planets in new ways, so your system stays alive, generative, and unmistakably yours.

The chapters ahead move us from mapping your orbit to viewing it through nine ancient lenses — Mercury through Pluto. Each planet carries its own story, its own science, and its own symbolic quality.

Together, they offer fresh ways of seeing your Sun and planets, so your system never runs dry.

Mercury – The Messenger

Hours old and already causing trouble. That's Mercury for you. According to Greek mythology, Hermes was born at dawn in a cave. By noon, he had invented the lyre. By evening, he had stolen fifty sacred cattle from his brother Apollo, walking them backwards to throw Apollo off the scent. When Apollo caught up with him anyway, furious, Hermes didn't fight. He played the lyre. The music was so beautiful that Apollo forgot his anger entirely and traded the whole herd for the instrument on the spot.

Born in the morning, inventor by lunch, cattle thief by dinner, deal-maker by nightfall.

What makes this story worth telling here is that Hermes was the god who could translate between worlds. He carried messages, guided souls, brokered deals no one else could. His gift was making connections others couldn't see, and making them quickly.

When the Romans adopted him, they named him Mercury, and gave his name to the planet closest to the Sun: a world that completes its orbit in just 88 days, enduring wild extremes of heat and cold, adapting constantly and never slowing down.

That is Mercury energy. Speed, yes. But also translation. Clarity. The ability to take something complex or hidden and make it land.

In Solar System Marketing®, Mercury represents your communication: your voice, your clarity, and the speed with which you create impact.

Speed itself is valuable currency. Mercury reminds us that value often lies in how swiftly we help others see, feel, or act. The clearest voice often wins, because it's the easiest to understand.

You've felt Mercury energy in your business already, even if you didn't name it that way. It's the moment in a conversation when you distil a complex idea into a single sentence, the other person's face changes, and they quote it back to you three months later. It's the speed with which you responded to a shifting market moment with timely, relevant insight that made people think, "They get it." It's a quick-fire FAQ on your website that answers the five questions every prospect asks first. It's a "one thing I'd tell you" post where you strip away all the caveats and just say the thing. It's the way you open a keynote with a single sentence that makes the whole room lean forward.

Mercury invites you to consider: How recognisably and clearly does your Sun shine through your words? How quickly does your audience grasp the benefit of what you do? How agile are you in adapting your message for different contexts?

When you filter your Sun or your planets through Mercury, new content angles emerge: What is my simplest, sharpest way of explaining what I do? How do I help people reach clarity or results faster than they could alone? If one of your planets is Systems, Mercury asks, "*How do I explain this process in thirty seconds or less?*" If one is Leadership, Mercury asks, "*What's the one sentence that captures my leadership philosophy?*"

Mercury energy tends to be lean, direct, and immediately useful. It's the kind of thing people repeat to a colleague. If you find yourself writing something and thinking, "I could say this in half the words," that instinct is Mercury talking. Follow it.

If Hermes were writing this chapter, he'd probably say: "*Say it faster. They already get it.*"

Think about the last time you cut through confusion for someone, when your words landed and something clicked into place. That was Mercury moving through you.

Reflection

Recall a moment when someone said, *"That was exactly what I needed to hear"* or *"You made that so clear for me."* What was the context, and what was present in how you communicated? Was it a presence, a passion, a belief?

Where in your work do you create speed: fast results, fast clarity, or fast connection?

Look at your solar system map. Which of your planets would benefit most from Mercury energy right now? What would it sound like if you explained that planet in a single sentence?

Venus – The Attractor

For centuries, people looked for a brilliant light at dawn, and another one at dusk. The Greeks called them the morning star and the evening star. But they weren't two stars. They weren't even one star. They were looking at Venus, wrapped in thick clouds that reflect sunlight so powerfully she outshines everything in the night sky except the Moon.

Sailors, poets, and lovers sought her out, drawn to her light without ever seeing what lay beneath it. They didn't need to. Her brightness comes from what she radiates outward. That's the lesson Venus carries into your marketing: attraction has less to do with revealing every detail and more to do with what you radiate.

In Solar System Marketing®, Venus embodies attraction, desire, and what makes your work magnetic to the right people. Your audience isn't moved only by logic. They're moved by desire, resonance, and the sense that what you offer will make their lives richer. Venus energy is what makes someone lean in and think, "I want that."

Samantha knows this shift intimately. A marketing leader with more than twenty years of experience, she was made redundant at the end of 2023 and faced the prospect of putting herself out there with a knot in her stomach. The instinct to perform, to push, to chase attention, felt deeply misaligned. As she put it, "I'm naturally not a self-promoter, so the idea of posting regularly felt quite daunting." So instead of forcing it, she turned inward. Through a values exercise, she discovered that respect, integrity and family sat at the core of everything she cared about. That discovery, she said, shaped everything about how she showed up. She found her true voice, and everything changed.

What happened next was pure Venus. Samantha began communicating from that place of alignment, and people noticed. Friends and colleagues told her it felt natural, authentic, and interesting. An ex-colleague, drawn in by what Samantha was sharing, reached out and referred her to a role. She got hired. Her presence carried a quality people wanted to move towards.

Two years later, Samantha returned to public visibility with greater confidence and even deeper alignment. This time her LinkedIn posts reached twenty to forty thousand impressions, with hundreds of likes. When she reflected on what changed, she described it simply: her communication had become much more aligned with her values and the things that mattered most to her professionally. That authenticity resonated with people. She never chased attention. She attracted it by being herself.

Venus energy shows up beyond content, too. It's the consultant people recommend to friends by saying, "You need to work with this person." It's the speaker who walks offstage and finds a queue of people wanting to talk, not because they have a specific question, just because they want to be in their energy. It's the founder whose passion for the work becomes something their team rallies around, the reason great people want to be part of it.

The words a client uses when they describe working with you to others tell you more about your brand than any survey could. Pay attention to that language. It's often the most honest marketing data you'll ever get. That was your Venus drawing them in.

Venus invites you to consider: What is the outcome or experience you create that people truly desire? What is the magnetism of your brand, the quality that draws people in without push? Pick one of your planets and ask, what makes this idea not just useful but desirable? If one of your planets is Innovation,

Venus asks, "How do I show its allure, the excitement of what's new?" If one is Community, Venus asks, "How do I make people feel they need to be in the room?"

Reflection

Think about the times someone said, "*I don't know what it is, but I just wanted to work with you.*" What was it? What were you doing, saying, or being in that moment that drew them in?

What do people most often say they love about working with you? Are you using their words in how you describe what you do?

Look at your solar system map. Which of your planets has the most natural pull? Which one makes people lean in when you mention it? That's where your Venus energy is strongest.

Earth – The Grounded Centre

In the 1970s, astrophysicist Michael Hart ran calculations to determine how far a planet could sit from its star and still support life. The margin was shockingly thin. Move Earth just 5% closer to the Sun and the oceans would eventually boil. Move it 5% further away and the whole planet freezes over. Five percent. That's the margin between everything and nothing. Scientists call this sweet spot the Goldilocks zone.

Within that range, not only does Earth support life, it supports such an astonishing variety of life, and not just above the ground. A single teaspoon of healthy soil contains more microorganisms than there are people on the planet. Billions of bacteria, fungi, and microscopic life forms, all working in the dark, unseen, unrecognised, and absolutely essential. Without them, nothing grows. No roots take hold. No seed becomes anything. The often invisible activity below the ground sustains everything the Earth produces.

That is Earth energy. The right conditions, held steady. And the quiet, unglamorous foundation that grows everything from them.

Earth energy in your marketing is about showing people how what you do creates solid ground beneath their feet. The conditions for the sustainable growth they're seeking. You don't overwhelm them with too much detail, too much work, or make it too hard. Nor do you leave them on their own. You sit right in the Goldilocks zone where they have enough information and support to grow towards their ideal outcome, but not so much that they feel swamped in the process. When your audience can feel that steadiness in how you communicate, they trust it. They come back to it. They build on it.

Your brand works the same way. The parts nobody sees, your rhythms, your systems, the way you follow up, the consistency of how you show up even when it feels like nobody's watching, that's the soil. Your clients rarely talk about the mechanics of how you work. They talk about how supported they feel. But without the soil, that feeling doesn't exist.

In my own work, when I support people to create a one-hour-a-week marketing process grounded in who they are and what they do, something shifts. They exhale. The marketing stops feeling like a chore, and starts feeling like a way of being.

The businesses that endure are the ones that feel solid. People return to them because they know what they'll get. There's a steadiness to Earth-centred work that builds trust over time, like topsoil forming. It's rarely glamorous, but it's what everything else grows from, because it creates the right conditions for the work to flourish.

Earth invites you to consider: How does what you do create the conditions for your clients to grow? Where do you bring complexity down to something someone can hold and use today? Pick one of your planets and ask, what would it look like grounded?

If one of your planets is Wellbeing, Earth asks, "How do I show people that what I offer isn't a quick fix, but a foundation they can build a life on?" If one is Culture, Earth asks, "How do I show people that a strong culture isn't built in offsites and manifestos, but in the small, consistent things that happen on a Tuesday?"

Reflection

When was the last time a client showed visible relief, when something finally made sense and they stopped spinning? What had you done or said to create that moment? That's Earth at work.

What do people keep coming back to you for? What is it about how you work that makes them feel supported?

Look at your solar system map. Which of your planets could help people build more sustainably, or feel more ease around what they do with you? That's where Earth energy wants to work.

Mars – The Drive

Mars looks red from Earth. It was named after the Roman god of war because of its blood-red colour. But the red isn't blood. It's rust.

Mars is red because its surface is covered in iron oxide. The planet has been exposed to the elements for aeons, and that exposure has left its mark. What looks like aggression from a distance is actually evidence of endurance. Of showing up, unprotected, for long enough that it changes how you look to everyone else.

Most of the people I work with aren't naturally combative. They don't want to pick fights or court controversy for its own sake. But the ones whose brands carry real weight, real presence, have something in common: they've been in the arena long enough for it to show. They've weathered the uncomfortable conversations, the moments where they said what they actually thought instead of what felt safe. And that exposure, over time, has given them a quality others notice. Earned boldness.

That is Mars energy. The drive to act, to endure, and to let the marks of that endurance become part of your presence rather than something you hide.

In Solar System Marketing®, Mars is your courage, your energy, and your capacity to act. Building anything worth having requires the willingness to fight for it. To endure friction. To stay exposed. Mars energy is what it takes to send the proposal, to raise the rate, to publish the piece that makes your stomach flip slightly before you hit post. If you have never felt a little uncomfortable putting your work into the world, you may not have let Mars do its job yet.

You probably know someone who spends months agonising over careful, balanced content, being sure not to offend anyone. (Maybe that person is you!) It performs fine. People like it. But nobody remembers it. Then one day they write something with a real position, stated with conviction. People disagree. A few unfollow or unsubscribe. And that single piece generates more inbound enquiries in a week than the previous three months of safe content combined. The friction is a signal that they're finally saying something worth responding to.

The software company I co-founded, Virtually Myself®, has a client, Josie, who consciously brings Mars energy into her writing when it's warranted.

She doesn't rant or critique without restraint. She knows that to land a point, she needs to communicate her firmly held opinion with earned conviction, without making people take up arms. Rust, not blood. Josie calls the writing style we developed with her the "subtle grenade," and it's incredibly effective.

Mars invites you to consider: Where does your brand show courage, saying what others avoid? Where are you holding back from taking a position because it might generate pushback?

Pick one of your planets and ask, what would it sound like if you said it with real conviction? If one of your planets is Purpose, Mars asks, "What do I believe so strongly that I'd say it even if half the room disagreed?" If one is Wellbeing, Mars asks, "What uncomfortable truth about this industry am I willing to name?"

Reflection

Think of a time you made a bold move before you felt fully ready. What pushed you to act, and what happened afterwards? That was Mars alive in you.

Where in your work do you feel most energised and passionate? What does that tell you about where your Mars energy naturally flows?

Look at your solar system map. Which of your planets needs more courage right now? Where have you been playing it safe? That's where Mars wants to work.

Jupiter – The Amplifier

In July 1994, astronomers watched something extraordinary. A comet called Shoemaker-Levy 9, broken into twenty-one fragments by gravitational forces, slammed into Jupiter over the course of six days. The impact scars were visible from Earth. Some of them were larger than our entire planet.

What made this remarkable wasn't the collision itself. It was what Jupiter had done before it. The comet had been drifting through the solar system on a trajectory that could have brought it much closer to the inner planets, to us. But Jupiter's gravitational pull captured it first. Pulled it in. Absorbed the blow.

Scientists have since calculated that Jupiter acts as a kind of gravitational shield for the rest of the solar system. Its mass is so enormous, more than twice the mass of all the other planets combined, that it routinely deflects or captures objects that might otherwise threaten Earth. Some researchers believe that without Jupiter, life on our planet might never have survived long enough to evolve.

The largest planet in the solar system protects the smallest ones. Its greatest contribution is what its size makes possible for everything around it.

The voices that carry the most weight in any industry are the ones that create a gravitational field around them, one that holds space, elevates others, and absorbs some of the impact so the people in their orbit can keep going. Real authority shelters.

That is Jupiter energy. Growth that protects. Presence that makes room. Authority that others feel safe to orbit around.

In Solar System Marketing®, Jupiter represents growth, authority, and amplification. This is where one-to-one expertise becomes one-to-many impact. The coach whose framework gets adopted by other coaches. The consultant whose article gets forwarded around a leadership team. The speaker whose phrase becomes shorthand in an industry. None of that happens because the person pushed harder. It happens because the idea had enough weight to travel on its own.

When does a message become a movement? When it stops needing you to carry it. Whether through publishing, speaking, teaching, or simply sharing ideas with enough clarity and generosity that they take on a life of their own, Jupiter is the lens that turns your core thinking into something with reach.

Jupiter invites you to consider: How does your work ripple outward, creating influence beyond direct results? How do you expand your presence in ways that feel generous and sustainable?

Pick one of your planets and ask, what would it look like amplified? If one of your planets is Storytelling, Jupiter asks, "How do my stories carry lessons that reach beyond the individual to the collective?" If one is Community, Jupiter asks, "How does my community become a gravitational field that draws in the right people?"

Reflection

Think about the times someone told you, "*I shared your idea with others.*" Your idea had enough gravity to pull someone else into its orbit, and they became a carrier of it. That's Jupiter at work.

Where do you naturally create a sense of abundance, generosity, or uplift in your work?

Look at your solar system map. Which of your planets has the most potential to travel beyond you? Which idea, if amplified, could take on a life of its own? That's where Jupiter energy wants to work.

Saturn – The Architect

In 1610, Galileo pointed his telescope at Saturn and saw something he couldn't explain. The planet appeared to have ears. Two strange bulges on either side that made no sense with anything he knew about the heavens. It took another 45 years before Christiaan Huygens confirmed what Galileo had glimpsed: Saturn was surrounded by a flat ring, suspended in space like nothing else in the known universe.

From a distance, those rings look like solid discs. Smooth, seamless, almost sculptural. One of the most beautiful and recognisable structures in the solar system.

Saturn's rings are actually billions of individual pieces of ice and rock, some as small as grains of sand, others the size of houses, all orbiting in precise formation. What looks like one elegant structure is really millions of separate pieces, moving in alignment.

Your brand works the same way. The people who look at your business from the outside and think "they've really got it together" are seeing the cumulative effect of countless small, deliberate choices, in alignment. The way you follow up. The rhythm of how you show up. The processes you've built, the boundaries you've set, the routines you protect. Together, they create something that looks effortless.

Saturn is the second largest planet in the solar system. Enormous, visually imposing, wrapped in those spectacular rings. Despite its vastness, if you put it in water, it would float.

That's worth remembering when you think about systems in your own work. The best structures don't feel heavy. They make things lighter. They're the reason you can show up on a difficult week without having to reinvent everything from scratch. They're why your client experience feels consistent even when your energy fluctuates. If your systems feel like they're weighing you down, they might not be the right systems. Saturn's lesson is that the right structure creates buoyancy.

In Solar System Marketing®, Saturn represents structure, discipline, and consistency. You create your cadence. You align all the pieces, whether as large as a house or as small as a grain of sand, to that cadence. Over time, your body of work becomes expansive and impressive, and effortlessly keeps your business above water. Working with you feels light to your clients, and to you.

Saturn invites you to consider: What structures or routines help you deliver consistently? What is the one thing people can always expect from you? And where is something out of alignment, creating drag? If one of your planets is Mindset, Saturn asks, "What daily habit would make everything else feel lighter?" If one is Strategy, Saturn asks, "Which part of this process is adding weight without adding value?"

Reflection

Think about the times someone said, *"I know I can always count on you for..."* That's Saturn at work.

Where can you show the discipline behind your results, the process that makes the outcomes possible?

What rituals or systems help you show up reliably, even when your energy fluctuates?

Look at your solar system map. Which of your planets needs a rhythm? That's where Saturn energy wants to work.

Uranus – The Innovator

On 13 March 1781, a musician-turned-astronomer named William Herschel spotted a faint, greenish disc of light drifting through his homemade telescope in a garden in Bath. He wasn't looking for a planet. He wasn't even a professional astronomer. He was a German-born oboist and composer who had taught himself optics and built his own telescopes in his spare time. When he saw the object, he reported it as a comet. It took weeks of argument among the astronomical community before anyone realised what he'd actually found: the first new planet in recorded human history, discovered in a back garden, through a handmade instrument, by someone nobody in the field had heard of.

One of the biggest discoveries in the history of astronomy was itself entirely unconventional. That feels right for the planet it revealed.

In myth, Uranus was the primal Greek god of the sky: boundless, unpredictable, the realm of pure possibility. Fittingly, it's the only planet named after a Greek god rather than a Roman one. Even the naming refused to follow convention. The planet lives up to that distinction. It rotates on its side, tilted roughly 98 degrees from its expected axis, rolling around the Sun like a ball while every other planet spins upright. Scientists believe a massive collision early in the planet's history knocked it sideways, and it never corrected course. It just kept going.

Sometimes your most original perspective comes from an impact you didn't choose: a career change, a failure, a moment that knocked you sideways and forced you to see everything from a completely different angle. The tilt became the defining feature.

In Solar System Marketing®, Uranus represents originality, disruption, and newness. Where are you willing to tilt, to do what no one else in your orbit is doing? Uranus energy brings breakthrough ideas, unexpected pivots, and the spark that differentiates you in a crowded sky.

That doesn't mean being polarising for the sake of it. Uranus energy at its best is purposeful strangeness: the kind that makes people stop, yes, but also the kind that makes them think differently about something that matters to them.

Uranus invites you to consider: What is the unconventional angle only you can bring to your

Sun? Where are you inspired to say something no one else has said yet?

Pick one of your planets and ask, what would it look like tilted? If one of your planets is Systems, Uranus asks, "How do I show the quirky hacks or unexpected twists that reinvent structure?" If one is Leadership, Uranus asks, "How do I challenge conventional leadership thinking with a fresh perspective?"

Reflection

Think about a time you tilted the lens and opened a new horizon for others. What had you seen that nobody else was talking about? That was Uranus at work.

Where in your work do people say, *"I've never heard it put that way before."* What made that moment possible?

Look at your solar system map. Which of your planets could use a tilt? Where are you following convention when your instinct is pulling you somewhere more original? That's where Uranus energy wants to work.

Neptune – The Dreamer

Astronomers in the 1840s noticed that Uranus was wobbling. Something massive and unseen was pulling it off course. Two mathematicians, working independently, calculated exactly where the mysterious influence must be. When observers pointed a telescope at the coordinates, there it was: Neptune, a world discovered purely by the effect it had on everything around it.

That is Neptune energy. Invisible influence. A pull so strong that people feel it before they can name it.

In Solar System Marketing®, Neptune represents vision, imagination, and storytelling. It asks: how do you invite people into a future they can't yet see? Neptune is the pull into possibility that you create. The imaginative depth, the vision, the picture of a world your audience hasn't yet visited but suddenly wants to inhabit.

Neptune asks you to do the work of translating what you know into what someone else can feel. A good metaphor makes an abstract idea land in someone's body. A well-told story lets your reader rehearse a future they haven't lived yet.

Neptune invites you to consider: What vision do you carry that others can step into? Where can you use storytelling to make the intangible tangible?

Look at your planets and ask, what picture could you paint with each one? If one of your planets is Innovation, Neptune asks, "How do I tell stories that make innovation feel magical rather than mechanical?" If one is Purpose, Neptune asks, "How do I tell the story of why this matters in a way that gives people goosebumps?"

Reflection

Think about the times someone told you, *"You helped me see what's possible."* Which of your stories or metaphors had painted that picture for them? That's Neptune at work.

What stories or metaphors do people carry with them after a conversation or after reading your work?

Where in your work do you most feel like a visionary, not just a problem-solver? That's where Neptune energy is already at work.

Pluto – The Transformer

In 2006, 424 astronomers voted to strip Pluto of its planetary status. Schoolchildren wrote protest letters. New Mexico passed a resolution declaring Pluto would always be a planet within its borders. People who hadn't thought about astronomy since primary school found themselves genuinely upset. Yet Pluto itself didn't change. It kept orbiting, kept shaping the Kuiper Belt, kept being exactly what it had always been.

The only thing that shifted was how we defined what was, and wasn't, part of our solar system. And in releasing the old definition, we made room for a richer understanding of what's actually out there.

In Solar System Marketing®, Pluto represents transformation, endings, and renewal. Definitions evolve, orbits change, sometimes people are going to get upset about it, but endings are simply the start of something new. Just as Pluto was redefined, we too are constantly asked to release what no longer fits so transformation can take place.

Perhaps you've had the experience of realising that the positioning you built your reputation on no longer fits. The way you describe what you do, the audience you speak to, the framework or service you built your work around. It served you well, and now it doesn't. The instinct is to quietly move on and hope nobody notices. But there's real power in showing your audience that your thinking is alive and still moving.

When you share the evolution of your understanding openly, something shifts. People trust you more, because they can see that your work has depth, that you're paying attention, that your solar system is a living system. Pluto was part of the solar system for seventy-six years until we realised it wasn't.

Pluto invites you to consider: What have you let go of in your work that created space for something better? How do you help your audience see that loss, change, or disruption can carry hidden gifts? Look at your planets and ask, which one has transformed since you first named it?

If one of your planets is Storytelling, Pluto asks, "How do I tell stories of transformation that honour both the shadow and the rebirth?" If one is Productivity, Pluto asks, "What am I still doing out of habit that's actually holding me back from the way I want to work now?"

I took the New Mexico route here. I included Pluto as a planet, then wrote a chapter about how it wasn't one. And that's fine. Within Solar System Marketing®, you get to define what is and isn't in your solar system. And so do I.

Reflection

Think of the times someone said, *"That change was hard, but it turned out to be a gift."* That's Pluto alive in your orbit.

When have you gone through a season of ending that later revealed hidden wealth? What did you have to release to find it?

Look at your solar system map. Which of your planets has already been through a transformation? What did it become on the other side? That's Pluto energy at work.

Looking Outward

Over the last nine chapters, you've collected a full set of planetary lenses: Mercury through Pluto. Each one offers a different way of seeing your Sun and your planets.

You can return to any lens at any time, shine it onto your Sun or any planet in your orbit, and find something fresh to say.

Now let's look beyond the planets, and explore what else a solar system has to offer people who are the brand.

PART V: BEYOND THE PLANETS

Eris & The Kuiper Belt – The Periphery

In 2005, astronomer Mike Brown found a small, icy body beyond Pluto, roughly the same size, and it caused absolute chaos. If this object existed, then either it was also a planet or Pluto wasn't one. The International Astronomical Union was forced to act, creating the category "dwarf planet" and stripping Pluto of the title it had held for seventy-six years. Brown named his discovery Eris, after the Greek goddess of discord, because one small object on the edge had thrown the entire system into chaos.

Eris now sits among the dwarf planets of the Kuiper Belt: a vast region of icy bodies, comets, and fragments stretching beyond Neptune. What we once thought was the empty edge of the solar system turned out to be crowded with countless objects, all orbiting in strange, tilted patterns. The periphery is never as empty as it looks.

In Solar System Marketing®, the Kuiper Belt is where your peripheral ideas live. These are the fragments that orbit nearby but never quite become part of your core. They're not planets. They don't carry enough gravitational weight to earn that status. But they keep showing up.

Think about the idea that keeps surfacing in your conversations with clients but doesn't fit neatly into any of your planets.

Maybe you keep getting asked about pricing strategy, but your planets are Storytelling, Community, and Creative Process. Pricing keeps orbiting. People keep bringing it up. You have thoughts on it. It just doesn't carry enough weight to be a planet in your system. It's a Kuiper Belt object.

Or consider a topic that once occupied a prominent place in your solar system but has lost its pull. You've changed. Your audience has changed. It's still out there, still part of your history, like a dwarf planet drifting at the edge of your orbit.

The work is to notice these fragments, honour them, and decide which stay as fragments and which you'll elevate into true planets. Some ideas will fade. Others will grow in gravitational pull until they earn their place in your system.

Keep an "observatory": a simple, ongoing list of your Kuiper Belt objects. Review it every quarter and notice what's drifting further out and what's drawing closer.

Reflection

Are there ideas you've outgrown, even if they once had planet status?

What's the one topic that keeps coming up in conversations but you haven't given a home to yet? Does it belong in your Kuiper Belt, or is it ready to become something more?

How can you keep track of what's floating on the periphery, so you notice what might be circling closer?

Constellations – The Personas

Depending on where you stand on the Earth, different constellations are visible to you. In Australia, the Southern Cross is the anchor of the night sky, so familiar it's on the flag. In the Northern Hemisphere, you'd never see it. You'd navigate by the Plough, or Orion's Belt. Same universe, completely different orientation, depending on where you're standing.

In Solar System Marketing®, constellations represent your audiences. Each audience stands in a different place, and from where they stand, they see your solar system differently. They notice different planets first. They respond to different language. They have different problems they're hoping your work will solve.

Constellations aren't part of your solar system. They don't orbit your Sun. They're the backdrop you orient to. Knowing which constellation you're facing tells you who you're speaking to and why.

Your Sun stays the same. Your planets stay the same. What shifts is which planet you foreground, which lens you use, and the language you choose, depending on which constellation you're facing.

Let's say your Sun is "Helping organisations achieve strategic clarity" and one of your planets is "Simple Systems and Structures." Now imagine two constellations: a solo consultant just getting started, and a startup founder scaling a small team.

When you're oriented toward the solo consultant, your planet might sound like: "You don't need a complicated marketing plan. You need three things you can do consistently this week without burning out. Let's map what's already working and build from there."

When you're oriented toward the startup founder, that same planet might sound like: "Your team is growing faster than your systems. If your marketing depends on you remembering to do it, it won't survive the next hire. Let's build a structure that runs without you running it."

Same planet. Same Sun underneath it all. Completely different framing, tone, and entry point. The solo consultant needs to feel capable. The startup founder needs to feel organised. That's the power of knowing which constellation you're facing.

Reflection

Are you clear on the language for how you speak to your different audiences?

Can you name your primary constellations, and do you know what each one needs from you first?

Moons – The Stabilisers

Since the dawn of time, the Moon has been a symbol of rhythm and renewal. Waxing and waning, marking time, guiding rituals. Farmers planted by its phases. Calendars were set by its cycles.

In Solar System Marketing®, moons represent the rituals, tools, and supports that keep your orbit steady.

Rhythm moons keep your cadence. A weekly reflection where you review how you showed up and what landed. A monthly check-in where you ask whether your planets still feel alive. A quarterly reset where you zoom out and look at the whole system.

Support moons keep you accountable. A trusted peer group you meet with fortnightly. A mentor you check in with each month. A colleague who will tell you honestly when your message is drifting.

Tool moons keep things visible. A content planning board where you can see your pipeline. A template you return to for writing or preparing talks. A simple tracker that shows which planets you've given attention to recently and which have gone quiet.

The beauty of moons is that they're entirely within your control. You can't always control how your work lands or whether a new offer gains traction. You can control whether you pause each month to reflect. Moons are the part of the system that holds steady even when everything else is in motion.

Reflection

What rituals and rhythms do you already have in place that keep your work steady? What's one that's missing?

Where does your system wobble when your rituals and rhythms aren't in place?

What's one ritual or rhythm you could start this week to bring more steadiness to how you show up?

Wormholes – The Connection Points

In myth and in fiction, there have always been magical doorways. The wardrobe that opens into Narnia. The looking glass Alice steps through. Bifrost, the rainbow bridge connecting worlds in Norse mythology. These aren't just plot devices; they're expressions of something we instinctively understand: that two places which seem impossibly far apart can sometimes be connected by a single, unexpected threshold.

In Solar System Marketing®, wormholes are those thresholds. They're the bridges between your planets, the surprising linkages that reveal new meaning. Wormholes are where insight happens: the moment when two seemingly separate ideas suddenly belong together.

A wormhole in action looks like this. Say two of your planets are "Storytelling" and "Simple Systems." On the surface, they don't obviously connect. Then you notice something: the reason most people struggle with content isn't a lack of stories; it's that they have no system for capturing them. That insight is the wormhole. From that single connection, you could generate an article about why a story bank beats inspiration every time, a workshop exercise walking people through a simple weekly story capture ritual, and a newsletter exploring why the most prolific storytellers are actually the most systematic. Two planets, one wormhole, multiple pieces of content across different formats. That's the kind of multiplication wormholes make possible.

The trick is paying attention. Wormholes tend to show up mid-conversation, in a question someone asks at an event, in a collaboration that seems unrelated until it isn't.

Reflection

What could be a natural but surprising bridge between two of your planets? What story could connect them?

Pay attention this week to where two ideas, conversations, or projects unexpectedly connect. These are often wormholes trying to open.

What wormhole between your planets could become the basis for a talk, a workshop, or a piece of writing?

Flying Objects – The Distractions

In 1986, the world was obsessed with Halley's Comet. It was my first year of high school, and my science teacher Mr Brace could barely contain his excitement. It dominated the news, the newspapers, every conversation. People who ordinarily couldn't name a single planet were suddenly planning where they were going to watch it from and buying binoculars they'd never use again. The comet only passes Earth once every seventy-five years, so for most people this was their one and only chance to see it. Special viewing events were organised across the country. When it finally arrived, millions looked up, squinted, said "is that it?", and went home. Within weeks, everyone had gone back to life as usual. The binoculars went in a drawer. Even Mr Brace eventually stopped talking about it.

That same pattern plays out in our businesses more often than we'd like to admit. A new platform launches and suddenly everyone's scrambling to be on it. A viral content challenge sweeps through your industry and you feel the pull to jump in. A competitor pivots to embrace a trending type of video and you wonder if you should too. Each one blazes across your field of vision, bright and urgent, and each one pressures you to react.

Some of these moments are genuinely worth paying attention to. Most are Halley's Comet moments: dazzling, brief, and ultimately not part of your system. The key characteristic they share is this: none of them have enough mass to hold a stable orbit. They're passing through.

In Solar System Marketing®, flying objects represent distractions, fads, and passing trends. They may be tempting, but without real weight they scatter your focus. The discipline is in discerning what belongs in your orbit and what's just passing through.

Most of us don't set out to chase trends. It happens gradually. You see something gaining traction, feel a flicker of excitement or anxiety, and before you've thought it through, you're halfway into a new initiative that has nothing to do with your Sun. Some common patterns worth recognising:

The Shiny Object Spiral. You spot a new platform, format, or topic and immediately start planning content around it, before asking whether it connects to any of your planets. Two weeks later, you've produced a flurry of topic ideas that don't fit anywhere in your solar system, and you've lost momentum on the work that does.

The Fear-of-Missing-Out Pivot. Someone in your industry announces a bold move and you feel a gut-level worry that you're falling behind. You start second-guessing your own orbit, even though it was working perfectly well yesterday.

The Audience-Pleasing Detour. A piece of content unexpectedly performs well on a topic that sits outside your system. You chase the engagement, producing more of the same, only to find that the audience it attracted doesn't convert, doesn't stay, and doesn't care about your actual work.

If you recognise yourself in any of these, your system is probably leaking energy to flying objects.

Next time something new catches your attention, run it through these questions: Does this connect to my Sun? Does it relate to at least one of my planets? Can I see myself still talking about this in six months?

If the answer is yes across the board, it might be a new planet worth exploring. If it only has sparkle, let it be what it is: a beautiful, brief streak of light.

Reflection

Which ideas tempt you with sparkle, but lack gravity?

How do you protect your orbit from being pulled off-course?

What would you do with the time and energy you'd get back if you let the flying objects pass?

Black Holes – The Cautionary Lens

In 1915, Karl Schwarzschild solved Einstein's field equations from the trenches of the Russian front and predicted a point in space where matter could collapse so completely that nothing, not even light, could escape. Einstein thought the idea was too extreme to exist in nature. For fifty years, most physicists agreed. Then astronomers began noticing stars orbiting invisible companions, gas spiralling into apparent voids and heating to millions of degrees before vanishing. The black holes themselves were invisible. They could only be detected by their effects: the wobble of nearby stars, the energy that disappeared.

That's exactly how the most dangerous drains on your marketing energy work. You rarely see them directly. You recognise them only by their effects.

In Solar System Marketing®, black holes are the places where your marketing energy collapses. You keep producing, pouring effort in, but nothing comes back. It might be a channel that never reaches the right audience, a client that drains all your creative energy, or a pattern of over-customising until your Sun disappears.

There are three warning signs to watch for. All give, no return: you invest but see no lift in presence, clarity, or opportunity. The more energy you put in, the heavier it feels: instead of momentum building, you feel increasingly stuck. Your core message gets diluted or buried: instead of amplifying your Sun, the activity scatters or hides it.

The work is to recognise these pulls early, before they consume the energy you need for the work that matters. Astronomers talk about "escape velocity," the speed an object needs to break free of a gravitational pull. Your marketing black holes need the same kind of decisive force. Drifting won't get you out.

Be honest about where your energy is going, name the channels, commitments, or patterns that consistently take more than they return, and redirect that energy toward something that genuinely amplifies your Sun. The earlier you recognise the pull, the less escape velocity you need.

Reflection

What would you stop doing tomorrow if you were honest about what's pulling you in?

What activity are you quietly hoping someone gives you permission to stop?

Is there something you are doing out of obligation that you'd never start if you were beginning today?

PART VI: BRINGING IT BACK DOWN TO EARTH

What holds your Solar System Together

Throughout this book, three forces have been at work.

Every time we talked about your Sun drawing the right people toward you, that was *attraction*. Every time we explored how your planets extend your reach and help your message travel, that was *amplification*. Every time we returned to coherence, to the importance of staying true to your centre, that was *alignment*.

These three forces are what hold your solar system together.

Attraction is the pull that makes your presence magnetic. It's what happens when your Sun is clear and your energy is congruent. When attraction is working, people find you and feel something. They stay. They pay attention. They tell others, *"You need to work with this person."*

Amplification is the force that helps your message travel further than you alone could carry it. Your planets do this naturally. Something you said on a podcast becomes a quotable moment, becomes a conversation starter, becomes a client enquiry.

Alignment is your solar system in sync. The same voice, the same values, the same commercial intent running through everything, whether someone finds you online, hears you speak, or sits across from you in a meeting. When your essence and your commercial focus are pulling in the same direction, people trust what they're experiencing.

You create the conditions for these three forces. A clear Sun creates attraction. Well-defined planets create amplification. Alignment comes from knowing who you are and letting that run through everything you do.

The remaining chapters are about making your system operational. Your messaging, your content, your planning rhythms, your capacity. This is where your solar system meets your real life, your actual week, your actual energy, your actual audience.

Marketing Messaging

Your audience will never see your solar system, but they will experience its effects. Your Sun gives your messaging consistency, while your planets give it variety. Rotate your communications through your solar system, and you'll stay on message without being repetitive.

Let's get specific, because this is the chapter where your solar system stops being a conceptual tool and starts becoming actual words on a page, in a pitch, on a slide, in a conversation.

Here's a pattern you can use again and again:

Sun statement + planet angle + audience need = message

Your Sun statement is the core truth you always come back to. Your planet angle gives it a specific flavour or entry point. The audience need grounds it in something your listener actually cares about.

Let's say your Sun is "helping leaders find their voice" and one of your planets is "executive presence." Your audience need might be "I freeze up in high-stakes meetings."

That gives you: "I help leaders find the words that match their authority, so they walk into any room knowing exactly what to say."

Now take the same Sun but rotate to a different planet, say "storytelling." Same audience, different need: "My presentations are technically solid but nobody remembers them."

"I help leaders turn their experience into stories that stay with people long after the meeting ends."

Same Sun. Different planets. Different messages. Both true. Both you.

This works everywhere.

Networking. Someone asks, *"So what do you do?"* Most people either ramble or recite a rehearsed elevator pitch that their latest favourite AI tool spat out. Instead, lead with your Sun and add one planet for texture. "I help leaders find their voice. A lot of that is about executive presence, how you show up in a room so that people hear your authority before you've finished your first sentence." The next conversation, you might rotate to a different planet and it sounds fresh again.

Presentations. Your Sun anchors your presentation commercially, but your planet gives it specificity and uniqueness. In workshops, you can rotate through different planets to keep energy high and perspectives varied. Your Sun holds the room together. Your planets keep it moving.

Digital content. Blog posts, newsletters, articles, videos, social media. Your planets give people different paths to find you, because each one is talking about a specific audience need and that makes you discoverable. They all make commercial sense because they shine a light back on your Sun. You stay front of mind without sounding like a robot.

Interviews. Media, podcasts, video, panels. Lead with your Sun and choose a planet for your examples or context. You'll never be caught off guard by a question, because your system gives you somewhere to go every time.

Meetings. Use your Sun as your anchor point, then let a planet expand the conversation. When the discussion starts to meander, your Sun pulls you back. When you need to go deeper on a specific point, a planet gives you somewhere to go.

You can draft dozens of variations across all of these. Each one sounds like you, because each one is built from the same core. None of them sound identical, because the planets keep shifting.

Your Sun gives you the anchor. Your planets give you infinite ways to express it.

Conversations as Content

One of the simplest ways to use your solar system is in the conversations you're already having. Every coffee chat, every boardroom discussion, every "What are you working on?" moment is an opportunity to bring your Sun and planets to life.

When you see your conversations this way, you stop treating "content" as something separate you sit down to create. Your everyday words become part of your orbit. The language you use with a colleague, a client, or a potential collaborator can easily become the language you share more widely.

You don't need to pre-plan which planet to use. Pay attention to who you're talking to and what they seem interested in. If they're asking about trends, lean into a planet that speaks to innovation or change. If they're sharing a frustration, reach for the planet that addresses that tension. The planet that's right is the one that meets the person in front of you where they are.

Over time, you'll get a feel for which planets land best with which audiences. That instinct is worth paying attention to, because it tells you something about which ideas carry the most energy.

The more you talk your solar system through, the more nuance emerges. You'll find yourself explaining a planet in a way you haven't before, or making a connection between two ideas that surprises you. When that happens, write it down. Even a few quick notes on your phone after a conversation can become the seed of a post, an article, or a workshop segment.

Pay attention to the moments when someone leans in, asks a follow-up question, or says "I've never thought of it that way." That's your content writing itself. Whatever you just said landed. If it landed in conversation, it will land in writing too.

A Cadence, Not a Calendar

One of the biggest struggles people face with marketing is consistency. The pressure to "post every day" or "stick to a content calendar" often leads to burnout or rigidity. Solar System Marketing® offers a different path: *rhythm over rules.*

A calendar tells you what to post on which day. It's a grid, and when life gets busy or your energy shifts, you fall behind, feel guilty, and sometimes abandon the whole thing. The psychological effect of "missing" something you'd scheduled isn't ideal for morale when you are the brand, both the message and the messenger.

A cadence is more like a flow. The question shifts from "What should I share today?" to "Which planet am I naturally orbiting right now? What's next in my sequence? What does my audience need to hear?"

A cadence allows for the ebbs and flows of life. Some weeks you'll have more to say. Some weeks less. What matters is that you always have something next in the queue. If something timely or more interesting comes up, talk about that. Your planets are lined up behind it, ready for when you need them. No blank page. No paralysis.

The order can shift. The timing can stretch or compress depending on your schedule. What stays consistent is that you're touching each planet regularly, and your Sun keeps anchoring everything. You're following a rotation, not a rigid grid. If your natural pace is weekly, go with that. If monthly feels more sustainable, that works too. The point is the rotation, not the speed.

And there's no rule that says you can only visit a planet once before moving on. If there's something you want to elaborate on, a series you want to explore, or a theme you want to sit with for a while, park on that planet for as long as it feels right. Then move on when you're ready.

The beauty of this approach is that it removes decision fatigue. You know which planet you're visiting and which style of delivery fits. The creative energy goes into the content itself rather than into the agonising question of what to talk about.

Reflection

Can you remember the last time you said something publicly about each of your planets?

Which planets get too much airtime, and which ones have you been quietly avoiding?

What rhythm feels honestly sustainable for you right now? Write down a rough cadence that matches your real life, not someone else's content strategy.

Check-Ins and Reviews

Your solar system isn't static. Just as the sky shifts with the seasons, your Sun and planets will evolve as your focus and energy change.

Every few months, pause and look at your system. Does my Sun still reflect what I'm offering now? Do my planets feel alive and connected, or are some ready to retire? Has my audience shifted, calling for a new emphasis or angle? Are flying objects pulling me off course?

These don't need to be long strategic retreats. A one-page review every quarter is often enough. Sketch your Sun, list your planets, and notice where energy is strong and where it has waned.

When you zoom out, you might see one of these.

Retiring a planet. A planet you once talked about passionately no longer lights you up. It was relevant to an earlier stage of your work, or you've simply said everything you needed to say about it. Let it drift to the outer edges of your orbit. Stop feeding it energy, and over time it will cool naturally.

Promoting a theme. You notice something that keeps showing up in your work but hasn't been recognised as a planet. It surfaces in your talks, your client conversations, your writing. Give it a name. Place it in your orbit. Start creating around it deliberately.

Recognising your Sun has shifted. This happens less often, but when it does, it's worth pausing for. Your Sun might shift when your business model changes, when you move into a new area of expertise, or when what you're known for evolves. The essence often stays the same, but the way it shines will change. When you sense this happening, update the language so it reflects where you are now.

Clearing the flying objects. Your review might reveal that you've been pulled off course by things that looked like planets but were really just passing debris. Name them. Let them go.

Every so often, pull back far enough to see your whole solar system at once. That perspective is where the best decisions come from.

Aligning Impact and Opportunities

A clear solar system doesn't just help you communicate. It helps you decide.

When your Sun and planets are defined, they become a filter for which opportunities to pursue and which to release.

Being visible is one thing. Being visible for the right thing is another. The more aligned your visibility, the more it compounds into credibility, and credibility is what opens the right doors.

A simple way to test any opportunity: Does it connect back to my Sun? Does it light up one of my planets? Does it drain or energise me? Energy is often the most honest indicator.

Say your Sun is "Helping leaders find their voice" and your planets include Executive Presence, Storytelling, and Resilience. You get an invitation to speak at a leadership conference on building capability in high-growth startups. Does it connect to your Sun? Yes. Does it light up a planet? Executive Presence and Resilience are both relevant. Does it energise you? You've been wanting to reach younger founders. Green light.

Same week, a former colleague asks if you'd co-facilitate a workshop on personal productivity hacks for freelancers. The pay is decent. The audience is big. Does it connect to your Sun? Not really. Does it light up a planet? You could make it fit, but honestly, it's a stretch. Does it energise you? When you imagine yourself in that room, you feel flat. That's a no. A kind, clear no.

For consultants and experts, the hardest part is often the no. Especially when the opportunity comes from someone you respect, or feels like it might not come around again. But saying yes to something outside your orbit has a cost. It takes time, capacity, and energy away from the opportunities that will move you forward in the direction you actually want to go.

A kind, clear no doesn't need to be complicated. "Thank you for thinking of me. This isn't quite in my area of focus right now, but I'd love to recommend someone who'd be a great fit."

Every no frees up capacity for a better yes. One that's aligned with your Sun and strategic for where you're heading.

The Living System

Your solar system is a living system.

You are the brand. And you are not the same person you were three years ago, or even last year. You've had seasons of growth, seasons of rest, moments that changed how you see your work.

Your solar system evolves because *you* do. The way you talk about what you do, the planets that light you up, the audiences you want to reach, all of it shifts as you shift. That evolution is the sign of a living brand.

It shifts with the seasons of your life, the changes in your work, and the evolution of your audience. What feels central today may become peripheral tomorrow. What begins as a fragment on the edge may eventually gather enough weight to become a planet.

This is where the real work of being a person brand lives. You build the system, yes. Then you orbit through it. Pay attention to what has gravitational pull.

The three forces evolve with you.

Attraction, in the early days, comes from specificity. Your Sun is new, your message is focused, and the right people find you because you're saying something distinct.

As your system matures, attraction deepens. People aren't just drawn to a focused message; they're drawn to a consistent one with depth behind it.

Amplification starts as reach. Your planets help your message travel to different audiences, different contexts, different formats. You're finding out which planets resonate and which fall flat.

Over time, amplification becomes about depth. Your planets have their own gravity now. People know you for specific ideas. They reference particular planets when they recommend you.

Alignment starts as discipline. You're checking: does this planet actually orbit my Sun? Does this opportunity fit? Am I staying true to my centre?

Over time, alignment becomes instinct. You feel it when something is off-orbit before you can articulate why. You notice faster when a new opportunity is a flying object rather than a genuine addition to your system.

Hold your system lightly. Orbit through it, yes. Check in regularly, yes.

Don't hold it so tightly that it can't evolve.

The whole point of building a solar system is that it can move with you.

When you let it, it will.

Setting It In Motion

You now have a complete way of seeing yourself, your work, and your marketing as one connected system.

A Sun at the centre. Planets that orbit with purpose. Lenses that open new perspectives. Supporting forces that keep you steady. And three forces, Attraction, Amplification, and Alignment, that make the whole thing work.

The final step is simple: begin.

Set aside thirty minutes.
Sit down with a blank page and create your first working version.

Your Sun, in one sentence.
Write down your commercial focus right now. One line. If it takes you more than a sentence, you're overcomplicating it.

Map your planets.
List seven to ten big ideas that orbit that Sun. These are your recurring themes, the things you talk about in client conversations, on calls, at dinners. You already know what they are.

Your first few weeks of content.

Pick a planet, choose a format, and create something. Then pick another. You'll quickly feel the rotation start to work. Each planet gives you a fresh angle, and they all lead back to your Sun.

Your review ritual.

At the end of each month, spend fifteen minutes checking in. Which planets got attention? Which ones did you neglect? Has anything shifted? Does your Sun still feel right? This is how you keep the system alive.

Your first version won't be your final version. That's the point. Just begin.

If you'd like support building your system, the next section shares tools and resources I've created to help.

APPENDIX

Next Steps & Resources

This book has given you the framework, the thinking, and the tools to map your own solar system and bring it to life. You can absolutely take what you've learned here and run with it. Everything you need is already in your hands.

For printables, resources, and bonus materials to help you work through the exercises in this book, visit **www.solarsystemmarketing.com**

When I first developed Solar System Marketing®, I used it for myself. Then I started teaching it to clients. The framework clicked quickly, but the implementation took time. Life got busy. Planets stayed half-developed. There was a gap between the strategy on paper and getting ideas into the world.

Together with my co-founder Alex Hagan, we built something to close that gap. Virtually Myself® is the done-for-you version of everything in this book. We work with you to define your Sun, map your planets, and build out your entire solar system. In practice, that looks like:

- A completed Solar System: your Sun, planets, and orbits, all mapped, defined, and ready to use

- A personalised content vault built from your own intellectual property, stories, and frameworks

- A voice-trained writing tool that generates content per your preferred cadence, from your vault, and whenever you need it

- Ongoing support to keep your system evolving as your business does

If you'd like to go from framework to execution with support behind you, visit www.virtuallymyself.com to find out more.

Acknowledgements

To Alex, my co-founder and partner in building Virtually Myself®, who saw what I saw from the evening the idea of Solar System Marketing® was born, and has been on this journey with me ever since. From the earliest conversations where it took shape, through the business where it came to life, and through every stage of it becoming a book. Thank you for always leaning into my myriad ideas, stoking the fire of my enthusiasm, and for helping me get this powerful idea out into the world. Here's to always looking at the stars, and all that unfolds from here.

To Rowena, who sparked the idea of me writing a second book and created a beautiful space for us to write our books alongside each other. And for your friendship and constant encouragement. You are a beautiful constellation in my universe!

And to my Marketing Me® and Virtually Myself® clients, who adopted the Solar System Marketing language so naturally and so quickly. You showed me just how user-friendly this concept is. Watching you instinctively start speaking in Suns and planets, and seeing how easily it became part of how you think and talk about your work, helped me see just how alive and ready this idea was. I'm so grateful to you all.

About the Author

If we're meeting for the first time, I'm so glad you're here. And honoured that you've read this book.

What I've learned from over 30 years working across brand, marketing, and leadership is that the most powerful marketing asset any business has is the person behind it. Their thinking, their story, their point of view. When that's clear and well expressed, everything else works harder.

I saw this play out during the two decades I spent running my own marketing agency (recognised as *Best Marketing Agency* at the Australian Marketing Excellence Awards in 2018).

It was around then, after twenty years on the frontline of business marketing, that I could see a big shift. People (not just founders) were becoming their own brands, and I wanted to take everything I'd learned about brand and strategy and apply it in a more personal, direct way. So I went all in, working with experts and founders as a strategist and mentor, helping them do for themselves what I'd spent years doing for brands. Including, eventually, my own. That work became Marketing Me®.

More recently, I co-founded Virtually Myself®, where I get to bring together my expertise in brand, positioning, and content with the technology that's reshaping how experts show up. Elevating positive voices of influence is such important work that the world needs right now.

I've been deeply embedded in the marketing profession, both as a practitioner and as someone who cares about where it's heading. As a Certified Practising Marketer (CPM), Fellow, and Life Member of the Australian Marketing Institute, I love being part of communities of stellar marketers globally who are shaping what good marketing looks like.

My mind has always been tuned to what's around the corner - seeing what's coming, spotting patterns, and translating them into something genuinely usable and impactful. My happy place is sharing all of that with people who are doing good work in the world, so they can adapt, stay ahead, and be ready for what's next.

As "people" brands, we are more than what we do professionally. I'm a mum to five, which means much of this journey has happened alongside hands-on parenting. That's given me a firsthand, personal understanding of why we need to fiercely protect our capacity, our health, our energy. It's the reason my entire personal brand ethos is built around having a doable, enjoyable plan you can execute in an hour a week or less.

Because if it doesn't work with your life, it doesn't work.

How This Book Came to Be

I know what it's like to step out from behind a company brand and build a personal one from scratch. I've done it myself. I went from being known through my agency and the social impact initiatives I'd founded along the way, to having to figure out how to show up as *me*, with my own voice, my own point of view, my own visibility. It was uncomfortable, messy, and one of the best things I've ever done.

That lived experience became the foundation for everything I now teach. I built Marketing Me® as a framework for personal branding and positioning, and began mentoring others through the same transition I'd navigated. But the benefits extended far beyond better marketing. Something shifted in people. A renewed passion for their work, their purpose, even their life.

My first book, *Marketing Me: Take Charge of Your Personal Brand and Make Your Mark on the World,* was born from that shift. It helped professionals uncover their identity as a brand, embrace what makes them distinctive, and express it with confidence and commercial clarity.

But the question that kept coming up was a practical one: "*I know I need to share more, but it takes so much time and effort to do it well.*" And that's true. Most experts and founders don't have a marketing strategist on hand 24/7. They need a simpler, more intuitive way to plan and share their thinking, and a way to more meaningfully use the tools now available to them.

The pursuit of an easier way is what led me to Solar System Marketing®, as a way to combine practicality with timeless, proven marketing principles.

I hope it lights something up for you the way it did for me.

If you enjoyed this book, I'd genuinely love to hear from you. Drop me a note at support@ninachristian.com and share your thoughts with me.

Work with Me

If this book has sparked something and you'd like to go deeper, here's how we can work together:

Marketing Me® - My mentoring and strategic advisory program for experts and founders who are redefining or elevating their positioning and want structured support, strategy and a clear runway for growth. Find out more at ninachristian.com/marketingme

Virtually Myself® - The end-to-end content system and intelligence infrastructure for founders, experts, and consultants who want to build influence by sounding like themselves at scale. We don't just create content. We protect what makes it valuable in the first place, and the ability to turn it into sustained demand. Find out more at virtuallymyself.com

Speaking and Workshops - I speak at conferences and run in-house sessions on personal branding, future-ready marketing, and the human side of being a visible leader in an AI-shaped marketplace.

For media enquiries, speaking engagements, or conference bookings, please contact support@ninachristian.com.

169